ANNA DEL CONTE

Italian

Anna Del Conte
Italian

Photography by Philip Wilkins

WEIDENFELD & NICOLSON

Anna Del Conte

Anna Del Conte was born in Italy and educated at the University of Milan, where she studied history. In the 1950s she married an Englishman and has lived in London ever since.

The *Financial Times* has described Anna as 'Britain's most respected writer on Italian food'. Among her widely praised books are *Portrait of Pasta* and the reference book *Gastronomy of Italy*, for which she was awarded the Duchess Maria Luigia di Parma prize in 1988. Her more recent books include *Secrets from an Italian Kitchen, Entertaining all'Italiana, Anna Del Conte's Italian Kitchen* and *The Classic Food of Northern Italy*, which won the 1996 Guild of Food Writers Book of the Year award in Britain; in Italy it won the Founder's Prize of the Accademia Italiana della Cucina.

Photograph by Martin Brigdale

Contents

RISOTTO CON LE COZZE 10
RISOTTO WITH MUSSELS (VENICE, NORTHERN ITALY)

SPAGHETTI COI PEPERONI ARROSTITI 12
SPAGHETTI WITH GRILLED PEPPERS (PUGLIA, SOUTHERN ITALY)

GNOCCHI ALLA ROMANA 14
SEMOLINA GNOCCHI (ROME, CENTRAL ITALY)

ORECCHIETTE COI CECI 16
ORECCHIETTE WITH CHICKPEAS (PUGLIA, SOUTHERN ITALY)

NASELLO ALLA SIRACUSANA 18
BAKED HAKE WITH ANCHOVY SAUCE (SICILY, SOUTHERN ITALY)

TRIGLIE ALLA MARCHIGIANA 20
RED MULLET WITH PROSCIUTTO AND ROSEMARY (MARCHE, CENTRAL ITALY)

MAIALE AL LATTE 22
LOIN OF PORK BRAISED IN MILK (EMILIA-ROMAGNA, NORTHERN ITALY)

POLENTA PASTICCIATA IN BIANCO 24
BAKED POLENTA WITH CHEESES (PIEDMONT, NORTHERN ITALY)

CAPONATINA 26
AUBERGINES IN A SWEET AND SOUR SAUCE (SICILY, SOUTHERN ITALY)

FINOCCHI STUFATI **28**
STEWED FENNEL (TUSCANY, CENTRAL ITALY)

TORTA DI RICOTTA **30**
RICOTTA CAKE (LAZIO, CENTRAL ITALY)

PRUGNE SCIROPPATE AL FORNO COL GELATO DI MASCARPONE **32**
PLUMS IN SPICED WINE WITH MASCARPONE ICE CREAM
(LOMBARDY, NORTHERN ITALY)

THE BASICS

   BATTUTO E SOFFRITTO 34

   POLENTA 34

   COOKING PASTA 35

   SAUCES 37

   TOMATO SAUCE 37

I like all simple things, boiled eggs,

oysters and caviare, *truite au bleu*,

grilled salmon, roast lamb

(the saddle by preference),

cold grouse, treacle tart and rice pudding.

But of all simple things, the only one

I can eat day in and day out,

not only without disgust

but with the eagerness of an appetite

unimpaired by excess, is macaroni.

SOMERSET MAUGHAM
FROM *THE HAIRLESS MEXICAN*

Introduction

The foundation of Italian cooking is home cooking. It is based on best quality ingredients, cooked in ways that will enhance and complement their flavour.

Because of the emphasis on fresh, and therefore local, ingredients, and because of the history of a country that was only unified just over a century ago, Italian cooking is highly regional. Of the 12 recipes chosen here, four come from the North, four from central Italy and four from the South. With them I hope to give an idea of the diversity of a cuisine which is simple and yet rich, healthy and yet full of flavour.

Most of the dishes are quite easy to make, although they still require care and – some of them – time. All of them call for top-quality ingredients. These are now widely available in the main branches of good supermarkets and, of course, in Italian delicatessens, where you will often find someone who can advise you, should you need it.

At the end of each recipe are a few suggestions as to how and when to serve the dish. I have usually placed these in the context of an Italian meal.

Anna Del Conte

Risotto con le cozze
Risotto with mussels

SERVES 4

1.5 kg/3 lb mussels
200 ml/7 fl oz dry white wine
1 litre/1¾ pints light fish stock
    or vegetable stock
5 tablespoons olive oil
1 onion, very finely chopped
salt and pepper
1 stick of celery, with the leaves
    if possible, finely chopped
1 garlic clove, finely chopped
350 g/13 oz Italian rice,
    preferably vialone nano
4 tablespoons chopped parsley,
    preferably flat-leaf

First clean the mussels. Scrape off the barnacles, tug off the beard and brush thoroughly with a stiff brush under running water. Throw away any mussel that remains open after you have tapped it on a hard surface.

Put the wine in a large sauté pan, add the mussels and cover the pan. Cook over high heat, shaking the pan occasionally, until the mussels are open, which will only take 3–4 minutes. Set aside a dozen or so of the best-looking mussels in their shells. Remove the meat from the remaining mussels and chop coarsely. Strain the cooking liquid through a sieve lined with muslin.

Heat the stock to simmering point and keep it just simmering all through the cooking of the risotto.

Heat the oil in a wide heavy saucepan, add the onion and a pinch of salt and sauté until soft. Add the celery and garlic and sauté for a further minute.

Add the rice and turn it over in the oil for a couple of minutes. Pour over the mussel liquid and stir well. When the liquid has been absorbed, you can begin to add the stock, a ladleful at a time. Stir very frequently. When the rice is cooked, draw the pan off the heat and stir in the chopped mussels. Taste and season with plenty of freshly ground black pepper, adding salt if necessary. Transfer to a warmed serving dish and top with the reserved mussels and the parsley. Serve at once.

In Italy risotto is always served as a first course, the reason being that it must be eaten the minute it finishes cooking. It is also quite usual to follow a fish first course with a fish main course. Red mullet (page 20) would be my choice. If you prefer meat or chicken, it should be simply cooked.

Spaghetti coi peperoni arrostiti
Spaghetti with grilled peppers

SERVES 4

4 large yellow or red peppers
400 g/14 oz spaghetti
2 garlic cloves, very finely sliced
100 ml/3½ fl oz olive oil
1 small dried chilli, seeded
    and crumbled
salt
3 tablespoons chopped fresh
    flat-leaf parsley

Place the peppers under a hot grill or on a wire rack directly over a gas flame. Cook, turning constantly, until the skin is black and charred all over. Peel off the burnt skin with a small sharp knife and then wipe the peppers with paper towels. Do not rinse the peppers under the tap, or the water will wash away the lovely juices. Cut the grilled peppers lengthways into strips.

Drop the spaghetti into rapidly boiling salted water and cook until al dente (page 35).

While the spaghetti is cooking, put the garlic and oil in a large frying pan and cook over medium–high heat for 30 seconds. Add the peppers and the chilli, reduce the heat and cook gently for 4 minutes, stirring occasionally. Add salt to taste.

When the pasta is ready, drain but do not overdrain and tip it into the frying pan. Sprinkle with the parsley and fry for a further minute, tossing constantly. Serve at once.

A typical southern Italian first course that can precede the baked hake (page 18), accompanied only by a salad, such as French bean and tomato salad. Finish with stewed fruits or a fruit salad. The grilled peppers also make a very good antipasto. Dress them with extra virgin olive oil, capers and anchovy fillets.

GNOCCHI ALLA ROMANA
Semolina gnocchi

SERVES 4

1 litre/1¾ pints full-fat milk
salt
225 g/8 oz semolina,
    preferably Italian
3 egg yolks
70 g/2½ oz Parmesan
    cheese, grated
pinch of grated nutmeg
100 g/3½ oz unsalted butter

Heat the milk with a pinch of salt in a heavy saucepan until just simmering. Add the semolina in a thin slow stream, beating rapidly with a fork or a whisk. Keep the mixture at simmering point and continue beating for about 10 minutes, until the semolina has formed a thick paste and can be drawn away from the sides of the pan.

Remove from the heat and leave to cool a little, then add the egg yolks, 2 tablespoons of Parmesan, the grated nutmeg, 25 g/1 oz of the butter and salt to taste. Mix well. Moisten a cold surface – marble or formica – with a little cold water, turn the semolina out on to it and spread to a thickness of 1 cm/½ inch. Leave to cool completely.

Preheat the oven to 200°C/400°F/Gas Mark 6. Using a 4 cm/1½ inch biscuit cutter, cut the semolina into rounds. (Moisten the cutter every now and then in cold water to make cutting easier.) Place the gnocchi in a buttered ovenproof dish large enough to fit them all in a single layer, slightly overlapping.

Melt the remaining butter in a small saucepan and pour over the gnocchi. Sprinkle with the remaining Parmesan and bake in the oven for about 15 minutes, until a light golden crust has formed. Leave to stand for 5 minutes before serving.

This delicate yet nourishing dish is a classic first course from Rome. It can be followed by any meat or fish dish as long as it is not heavy, and accompanied by green vegetables.

ORECCHIETTE COI CECI
Orecchiette with chickpeas

SERVES 4

1 leek, white and pale green
   part only
6 tablespoons extra virgin
   olive oil
350 g/13 oz orecchiette
   or fusilli pasta
salt and pepper
3 tablespoons chopped fresh
   flat-leaf parsley
1 garlic clove, chopped
½ fresh red chilli, seeded
   and chopped
400 g/14 oz canned chickpeas,
   drained

With the root end intact, cut the leek lengthways into very thin slices, no thicker than 5 mm/¼ inch, and then cut each slice thinly lengthways to form thin strands. Then cut off the root end so that the strands separate. Wash and dry these strands thoroughly.

Heat 1 tablespoon of the oil in a large frying pan. Add the leek strands and stir-fry for 3 minutes. They should be crisp but not brown. Remove from the pan with a slotted spoon and set aside.

Drop the pasta into rapidly boiling salted water and cook until al dente (page 35).

While the pasta is cooking, heat the remaining oil in the frying pan. Add the parsley, garlic and chilli and sauté for 1 minute. Mix in the chickpeas, a grinding of black pepper and salt to taste and stir-fry for 2 minutes.

When the pasta is ready, drain immediately and transfer to the frying pan. Stir-fry together for 1 minute, then pour into a warmed bowl. Scatter the leek strands over the top and serve at once.

A rustic first course that can precede a dish of grilled sardines or grilled sausages, both accompanied by a green salad. A menu more suitable for lunch than for dinner. The finale should be a platter of cheese – to include a wedge of Parmigiano-Reggiano – and a bowl of fruit.

NASELLO ALLA SIRACUSANA
Baked hake with anchovy sauce

SERVES 4

1 hake, about 900 g/2 lb
4 tablespoons olive oil
salt and pepper
2 sprigs of rosemary
½ lemon, cut into thin slices
5 salted anchovies, boned
   and rinsed, or 10 anchovy
   fillets, drained
1 garlic clove, finely chopped

To serve
boiled potatoes

Preheat the oven to 190°C/375°F/Gas Mark 5.

Wash the hake and dry well on paper towels. Brush a little oil inside the fish and season the cavity with salt and pepper. Stuff the rosemary and lemon slices inside and secure with cocktail sticks.

Heat the remaining oil in a small saucepan, add the anchovies and garlic and mash to a paste with a fork.

Lay a piece of foil, large enough to wrap the fish, on a baking sheet. Lay the hake on the foil and pour over the anchovy sauce, turning the fish over so that it is completely coated. Add a little salt and a generous amount of pepper. Seal the foil around the fish and bake for 30–35 minutes, until done.

Lay the parcel on an oval dish and open it at the table. Slice the fish into steaks and spoon around some of the cooking juices. Serve with boiled potatoes to soak up the delicious sauce.

No other vegetables are needed, possibly just a salad to follow. A minestrone or the gnocchi alla romana (page 14) would be a good starter. Both courses being quite substantial, the pudding could be light, an ice cream or sorbet in the summer, and a salad of caramelized oranges or fresh pineapple in the winter.

TRIGLIE ALLA MARCHIGIANA
Red mullet with prosciutto and rosemary

SERVES 4

4 red mullet, cleaned but with
  the heads left on
juice of 1 lemon
5 tablespoons extra virgin
  olive oil
salt and pepper
1 tablespoon chopped fresh
  rosemary
1 garlic clove, chopped
4 tablespoons dried
  breadcrumbs
4 large slices of prosciutto,
  not too thinly cut

To serve
2 lemons, cut into wedges

Lay the red mullet in a dish. Mix together the lemon juice and 2 tablespoons of the oil, add salt and pepper and spoon a little of the mixture into the cavity of each fish. Brush the rest of the lemon and oil mixture all over the fish and leave to marinate for 2 hours.

Preheat the oven to 190°C/375°F/Gas Mark 5. Brush an oven dish with a little oil.

Mix together the rosemary, garlic, breadcrumbs, a little salt and a generous amount of pepper. Coat the fish with the mixture, pressing the crumbs on to the fish with your hands. Wrap a slice of prosciutto around each fish and lay the fish in the oven dish. Drizzle with the remaining oil and bake for 15−20 minutes, basting the fish twice during cooking. Serve from the dish, handing round the lemon wedges and a little of your best extra virgin olive oil for a final blessing.

In Italy a dish of fish is served by itself, without vegetables, but with a salad to follow. Try a tomato, pepper and cucumber salad or a simple green salad. If you want to serve an accompanying vegetable I would suggest a bowl of spinach dressed with extra virgin olive oil and lemon juice. The meal can begin with gnocchi alla romana (page 14) or with most pasta dishes, a risotto or a soup. If the first course is filling, the ideal dessert would be a bowl of fresh fruit or strawberries or raspberries with cream. But if the first course is a light soup I would finish with your favourite chocolate mousse or my ricotta cake (page 30).

MAIALE AL LATTE
Loin of pork braised in milk

SERVES 6–8

1.5 kg/3 lb neatly tied loin of
pork, boned and rindless
but with a thin layer of fat
4 tablespoons olive oil
2 cloves, bruised
pinch of ground cinnamon
1 sprig of rosemary
2 garlic cloves, bruised
salt and pepper
6–7 peppercorns, bruised
1 bay leaf
50 g/2 oz unsalted butter
300 ml/10 fl oz full–fat milk

Put the meat in a bowl and add 2 tablespoons of the oil, the cloves, cinnamon, rosemary, garlic, 1 teaspoon salt, the peppercorns and the bay leaf. Coat the pork all over in the marinade, cover and marinate for about 8 hours. Turn the meat over whenever you remember.

Heat the butter and the remaining oil in a heavy casserole into which the pork will fit snugly. When the butter foam begins to subside, add the meat and brown well on all sides and on the ends.

Heat the milk to boiling point and pour slowly over the meat. Sprinkle with salt, place the lid over the pan slightly askew and cook for about 3 hours at a steady low simmer. Turn the meat over and baste approximately every 20 minutes. By the end of the cooking the meat should be very tender and the sauce should be a rich dark golden colour, and quite thick.

Transfer the meat to a carving board and cover with foil. If the sauce is still too thin, boil briskly without the lid until it darkens and thickens.

Skim off as much fat as you can from the surface of the sauce, add 2 tablespoons hot water and boil over high heat for about 2 minutes, scraping the bottom of the pan with a metal spoon. Taste and adjust the seasoning. Remove the string and carve the pork into 1 cm/ ½ inch slices. Arrange on a large warmed plate and spoon the sauce over the pork.

This winter dish really calls out for a buttery potato purée to mop up the sauce. A bowl of spinach would be my choice for a second vegetable. For a first course I suggest a light soup or a salad of celeriac.

Polenta pasticciata in bianco
Baked polenta with cheeses

SERVES 6

300 g/11 oz polenta
(coarse maize flour)
150 g/5 oz gorgonzola,
cut into small pieces
125 g/4 oz fontina,
cut into small pieces
125 g/4 oz taleggio,
cut into small pieces
70 g/2½ oz Parmesan,
freshly grated
½ teaspoon freshly
grated nutmeg
2–3 pinches of cayenne pepper
salt

Béchamel sauce
750 ml/1¼ pints full-fat milk
85 g/3 oz unsalted butter
70 g/2½ oz plain flour

Make the polenta following the instructions on page 34 and leave to cool, which will take at least 2 hours.

When cold, cut the polenta into slices no more than 1 cm/½ inch thick. Preheat the oven to 200°C/400°F/Gas Mark 6.

Make the béchamel sauce. Heat the milk to simmering point. Melt the butter in a saucepan and blend in the flour. Cook for 30 seconds or so and then draw off the heat and begin gradually to add the milk. When all the milk has been incorporated, put the pan back on the heat and bring to a simmer, stirring constantly. Continue cooking the sauce for about 10 minutes, either in a bain-marie (put the saucepan inside a larger saucepan of gently simmering water) or using a heat dispersing mat. Add the cheeses and stir until dissolved. Add the nutmeg and cayenne pepper, taste and add salt if needed.

Butter a large shallow oven dish into which the polenta will fit in three or, maximum, four layers. Spread 3–4 tablespoons of the cheese sauce over the bottom and cover with a layer of polenta slices. Continue with these layers, finishing with plenty of cheese sauce.

Bake for about 15 minutes, or about 25 minutes if the dish was cold, having been prepared totally in advance. The top should show patches of golden crust. Serve hot.

This is a winter dish, quite rich, which can be a first course, followed, in an informal dinner, by a light second course based on vegetables. Alternatively it can be a main course in a vegetarian meal, when a platter of roast vegetables or a vegetable mousse would be a good opening.

CAPONATINA
Aubergines in a sweet and sour sauce

SERVES 4

675 g/1½ lb aubergines, cut
    into 2.5 cm/1 inch cubes
salt and pepper
vegetable oil for frying
1 head of celery
85 ml/3 fl oz extra virgin olive oil
1 onion, sliced
225 g/8 oz canned plum
    tomatoes, drained,
    or fresh ripe tomatoes,
    skinned and seeded
1 tablespoon sugar
100 ml/3½ fl oz red wine vinegar
50 g/2 oz capers
50 g/2 oz large green olives,
    stoned and quartered

Sprinkle the aubergine cubes with salt and place them in a colander to drain. Put a weight on top and leave to stand for at least 30 minutes. Rinse the aubergines, then dry well on paper towels.

Heat 2.5 cm/1 inch of vegetable oil in a frying pan. When the oil is hot, add a layer of aubergines and fry until golden brown on all sides. Drain on paper towels. Repeat until all the aubergines are cooked.

Remove the outer sticks of the celery and reserve for another dish or to make stock. Remove any threads from the inner sticks. Wash, dry and cut into 2.5 cm/1 inch matchsticks. Fry the celery in the same frying pan as the aubergines, until golden and crisp. Drain on paper towels.

Pour the olive oil into a clean frying pan and add the onion. Cook gently for about 2 minutes, until soft and just coloured. Pass the tomatoes through the fine holes of a food mill and add to the onion together with the sugar, salt and pepper and cook over moderately high heat, stirring frequently, for 15 minutes. Then add the vinegar, capers, olives, aubergines and celery and cook, over very low heat, for a further 20 minutes, stirring occasionally. Taste and adjust the seasoning. Pour the caponatina into a serving dish and leave to cool. Serve at room temperature.

Caponatina is served with bread as a delicious antipasto. It could be followed by the loin of pork braised in milk (page 22), or by red mullet in prosciutto (page 20) or any other dish not too delicately flavoured. To end the dinner I suggest a fresh-tasting pudding based on fruit, such as a fruit tart.

FINOCCHI STUFATI
Stewed fennel

SERVES 4

3 large fennel bulbs or
    4 smaller ones
5 tablespoons extra virgin
    olive oil
about 150 ml/5 fl oz vegetable
    stock
salt and pepper

Trim the fennel, cutting off the stalks and paring away any brown parts. Keep the green fronds for decoration. Cut the fennel lengthways into quarters and then into wedges about 1 cm/½ inch thick, keeping some of the central core attached to each wedge to prevent them from breaking up during cooking. Place the fennel in a colander and wash. Dry thoroughly.

Heat the oil in a large sauté pan into which the fennel will fit in a single layer. When the oil is hot, add the fennel and sauté for about 7–8 minutes, stirring occasionally with a fork rather than a spoon, until the wedges are browned at the edge. Pour in enough stock to cover the bottom of the pan and season with a little salt. Cover the pan and cook gently for about 20 minutes, until the fennel is tender, not crunchy. You might have to add a little more stock during cooking. When the fennel is ready there should be just a few spoonfuls of liquid left.

If there is still a lot of liquid, transfer the fennel to a warmed serving dish and boil the liquid over high heat until syrupy. Add a generous grinding of pepper and then taste and adjust the salt. Sprinkle the fennel with the reserved snipped fronds.

A delicious accompaniment to roast or grilled fish, or to a dish of simply cooked poultry or meat such as steaks. This is a typical Italian method of cooking vegetables. Some vegetables, such as courgettes, do not need any added liquid; others, like French beans, may be blanched first.

TORTA DI RICOTTA
Ricotta cake

SERVES 4–6

(the quantities can be doubled for a 25 cm/10 inch diameter cake)

85 g/3 oz sultanas
70 g/2½ oz unsalted butter,
   at room temperature
150 g/5 oz granulated sugar
2 large eggs, at room temperature
grated rind of ½ organic lemon
3 tablespoons potato flour
1½ teaspoons baking powder
pinch of salt
450 g/1 lb fresh ricotta cheese
icing sugar

Soak the sultanas in hot water for 15 minutes to plump them up. Preheat the oven to 180°C/350°F/Gas Mark 4.

Beat the butter until creamy. Set aside 1 tablespoon of the sugar and beat the rest with the butter. Beat in the eggs, one at a time. When the eggs have been incorporated, mix in the lemon rind, potato flour, baking powder and salt. Pass the ricotta through the small hole disc of a food mill, or through a sieve, directly on to the other ingredients. Do not use a processor as this would not aerate the ricotta. Fold the ricotta thoroughly into the mixture.

Generously butter a 15 cm/6 inch diameter spring-clip tin and sprinkle with the reserved sugar. Spoon the ricotta mixture into the tin and bake for about 1 hour, until a small skewer inserted into the centre comes out clean. Leave to cool.

Unmould the cake when it is cold. Just before serving, sprinkle with plenty of icing sugar.

This is suitable for serving at the end of any meal, because it is quite light – much lighter than American-style cheesecake.

Prugne sciroppate al forno col gelato di mascarpone

Plums in spiced wine with mascarpone ice cream

SERVES 6

1 kg/2¼ lb firm ripe plums
300 ml/10 fl oz good red wine
about 200 g/7 oz caster sugar
1 sprig of rosemary
1 thin strip of lemon rind
  (the yellow part only)
2 cloves
1 cinnamon stick, about 5 cm/
  2 inches long
6 peppercorns, lightly bruised

Mascarpone ice cream
400 g/14 oz mascarpone cheese
125 g/4 oz icing sugar
3 large organic egg yolks
4 tablespoons amaretto liqueur

Wash the plums and lay them in a shallow oven dish just large enough to contain them in a single layer.

In a saucepan, heat the wine with all the remaining ingredients. Bring slowly to the boil, stirring constantly. Let it boil gently for 5 minutes, then set aside to infuse for at least 30 minutes. Preheat the oven to 160°C/325°F/Gas Mark 3.

Strain the syrup, reheat it and pour it over the plums. Cover the dish with foil and tie the foil under the rim of the dish. Bake in the oven for 20–30 minutes. Test after 20 minutes; the plums should be just soft and well plumped up. Lift one out and taste it; if necessary add a little more sugar, but bear in mind that the mascarpone ice cream is quite sweet. Serve warm or cold but not straight from the oven or the refrigerator.

To make the ice cream, put the mascarpone in a large bowl or a food processor, sift in the icing sugar and beat into the mascarpone, then beat in the egg yolks and amaretto. Spoon the mixture into the bowl in which you want to serve it, and cover with cling film. Freeze for at least 6 hours. Transfer to the refrigerator about 1 hour before serving.

This is quite a rich, yet palate-cleansing, finale to a dinner party. The main course could be the loin of pork braised in milk (page 22), a stew or chicken cooked in a tomato sauce or in wine.

The Basics

BATTUTO E SOFFRITTO

Battuto, literally 'beaten', in a culinary context means chopped so fine as to appear pounded. A battuto, consisting traditionally of chopped pork fat and/or pancetta, onion, garlic, parsley, celery and carrot, is the starting point for most Italian recipes for sauces, meat dishes and soups. The traditional *lardo* – pork fat – is now often replaced by oil.

The battuto becomes a soffritto by being subjected to a slow, careful frying, the result of which is to achieve the characteristic Italian taste.

There are three secrets of a good soffritto. Firstly the battuto should be very finely chopped. Secondly the soffritto should cook very gently, being carefully watched, and stirred quite frequently. The third secret is that when onion is the first ingredient to be sautéed you should add a pinch of salt to it at the beginning. The salt releases the moisture in the onion, thus preventing it from frying too quickly.

POLENTA

For 6 people, fill a large saucepan with 1.7 litres/3 pints water. Bring to a simmer and add 2 teaspoons salt. Remove from the heat and add 300 g/11 oz coarse maize flour, preferably 'Polenta Bramata', letting it fall into the water through the fingers of your clenched fist while with the other hand you beat with a large wooden spoon or a balloon whisk. When all the flour has been added, return the pan to the heat and cook at a lively boil for 40 minutes. Whisk constantly at first and then as often as you can between one short rest and the next. It is also possible to add the flour to hot water instead of boiling water. You can then add the flour more quickly because there is no risk of lumps forming.

POLENTA MADE IN THE OVEN

This is a less demanding way to make polenta and the result is very satisfactory. Preheat the oven to 190°C/375°F/Gas Mark 5. Proceed as before but only boil the polenta for 5 minutes. Transfer the polenta to a buttered oven dish. Cover with buttered foil and cook in the oven for 1 hour.

If you want to serve the polenta grilled, let it cool completely and then cut it into 1 cm/½ inch slices. Brush with olive oil and melted butter and then grill or place in a hot oven for 10 minutes.

PASTA: FRESH OR DRIED?

Italians consider dried pasta ideal for many sauces and would never regard it as merely a substitute for fresh pasta. Factory-made dried pasta is made from durum wheat ground into semolina and mixed with water. The 'fresh pasta' sold in specialist shops and super-markets is made with durum wheat semolina, flour, eggs and water, and though it is convenient, it certainly is not as good as homemade pasta, and compares badly with dried egg pasta of a good Italian brand.

COOKING PASTA

It is easy to cook pasta, but it can be spoiled by carelessness. Pasta needs to be cooked in a large saucepan and a lot of water – about 1 litre/1¾ pints for 100 g/3½ oz pasta. Bring the water to the boil and then add salt – about 1½ tablespoons for 4 litres/7 pints water, which is the quantity needed for 300–450 g/11 oz–1 lb pasta. Slide all the pasta into the boiling water, stir with a wooden fork or spoon to separate the pasta shapes, and cover so that the water returns to the boil as soon as possible. Remove the lid and adjust the heat so that the water boils briskly, but does not boil over. The pasta is ready when it is al dente, which means that it offers some resistance to the bite. It is unnecessary to add cold water to pasta after cooking it. The timing of cooking varies according to shapes; all fresh pasta cooks more quickly than dried pasta.

DRAINING PASTA

Pasta should be drained as soon as it is al dente. However, if the pasta is going to be cooked further, by baking or frying, or if it is going to be served cold, drain it when slightly undercooked.

It is important to drain pasta properly. Use a colander that is large enough to contain all the pasta. Tip the pasta in, give the colander two or three sharp shakes and immediately turn the pasta into a heated bowl or dish, into the frying pan with the sauce or back into the saucepan in which it has cooked. Penne, gnocchi or any shapes that are hollow need more draining because water may be trapped in the hollows. However, pasta should never be overdrained, as it needs to be slippery for coating with the sauce.

Many Italians do not use a colander for long pasta. The strands are lifted out of the pan with two long forks and kept in the air for only a few seconds for the excess water to run off. All pasta must be dressed as soon as it is ready. A few tablespoons of the water in which the pasta has cooked are added for some types of thick sauces, such as pesto or carbonara.

SAUCES

Classic Italian cooking has very few sauces and these are mostly dedicated to pasta. In general, long thin shapes are dressed with an olive oil-based sauce that allows the strands to remain slippery and separate. Thicker long shapes, such as bucatini and fettuccine, are best in heavier sauces containing prosciutto or bits of meat, cheese and eggs. Medium-size short tubular pasta like orecchiette and fusilli are perfect with vegetable sauces. Penne, maccheroni and other large tubular shapes are the perfect foil for a rich meat ragu and for use in most baked dishes.

TOMATO SAUCE

MAKES ABOUT 700 G/1½ LB,

ENOUGH FOR 450 G/1 LB PASTA

1 kg/2¼ lb ripe tomatoes,
   cut into quarters
1 stick of celery, strings
   removed, cut into pieces
1 onion, coarsely chopped
½ carrot, chopped
2 garlic cloves
3–4 sprigs of parsley
2 fresh sage leaves
1 sprig of thyme, leaves only
1 teaspoon tomato purée
1 teaspoon sea salt
1 teaspoon sugar
freshly ground black pepper
4 tablespoons extra virgin
   olive oil or
   50 g/2 oz unsalted butter

If you want to use a food processor you must peel the tomatoes before you start.

Put all the ingredients – except the pepper and the oil or butter – in a fairly wide saucepan and bring to the boil. Cook over lively heat for the first 10 minutes or so, while mashing the tomatoes down with a spoon. Turn the heat down and continue cooking for 40 minutes, stirring occasionally. By the end of cooking the sauce should be thick and the liquid should have evaporated.

Put the sauce through a food mill or a sieve, or blend in a food processor. Taste, add a generous grinding of pepper and adjust the salt.

For dressing pasta, add the oil or the butter. For other dishes, use as it is; it is handy for meat or vegetable stews, vegetable or fish soups, or fish dishes. You can make larger quantities and freeze it.

Classic Cooking

STARTERS

Lesley Waters A former chef and now a popular television cook, appearing regularly on *Ready Steady Cook* and *Can't Cook Won't Cook*. Author of several cookery books.

VEGETABLE SOUPS

Elisabeth Luard Cookery writer for the *Sunday Telegraph Magazine* and author of *European Peasant Food* and *European Festival Food*, which won a Glenfiddich Award.

GOURMET SALADS

Sonia Stevenson The first woman chef in the UK to be awarded a Michelin star, at the Horn of Plenty in Devon. Author of *The Magic of Saucery* and *Fresh Ways with Fish*.

FISH AND SHELLFISH

Gordon Ramsay Chef/proprietor of London's Aubergine restaurant, recently awarded its second Michelin star, and author of Glenfiddich Award-winning *A Passion for Flavour*.

CHICKEN, DUCK AND GAME

Nick Nairn Chef/patron of Braeval restaurant near Aberfoyle in Scotland, whose BBC-TV series *Wild Harvest* was last summer's most successful cookery series, accompanied by a book.

LIVERS, SWEETBREADS AND KIDNEYS

Simon Hopkinson Former chef/patron at London's Bibendum restaurant, columnist and author of *Roast Chicken and Other Stories* and *The Prawn Cocktail Years*.

VEGETARIAN

Rosamond Richardson Author of several vegetarian titles, including *The Great Green Cookbook* and *Food from Green Places*.

PASTA

Joy Davies One of the creators of *BBC Good Food Magazine*, she has been food editor of *She, Woman* and *Options* and written for the *Guardian, Daily Telegraph* and *Harpers & Queen*.

CHEESE DISHES

Rose Elliot The UK's most successful vegetarian cookery writer and author of many books, including *Not Just a Load of Old Lentils* and *The Classic Vegetarian Cookbook*.

POTATO DISHES

Patrick McDonald Former chef/patron of the acclaimed Epicurean restaurant in Cheltenham, and food consultant to Sir Rocco Forte Hotels.

BISTRO

Anne Willan Founder and director of La Varenne Cookery School in Burgundy and West Virginia. Author of many books and a specialist in French cuisine.

ITALIAN

Anna Del Conte Author of several books on Italian food, including *The Gastronomy of Italy, Secrets from an Italian Kitchen* and *The Classic Food of Northern Italy* (chosen as the 1996 Guild of Food Writers Book of the Year).

VIETNAMESE

Nicole Routhier One of the United States' most popular cookery writers, her books include *Cooking Under Wraps, Nicole Routhier's Fruit Cookbook* and the award-winning *The Foods of Vietnam*.

MALAYSIAN

Jill Dupleix One of Australia's best known cookery writers and broadcasters, with columns in the *Sydney Morning Herald* and *Elle*. Her books include *New Food* and *Allegro al dente*.

PEKING CUISINE

Helen Chen Author of *Chinese Home Cooking*, she learned to cook traditional Peking dishes from her mother, Joyce Chen, the *grande dame* of Chinese cooking in the United States.

STIR-FRIES

Kay Fairfax A writer and broadcaster whose books include *100 Great Stir-fries, Homemade* and *The Australian Christmas Book*.

NOODLES

Terry Durack Australia's most widely read restaurant critic and co-editor of the *Sydney Morning Herald Good Food Guide*. He is the author of *YUM*, a book of stories and recipes.

NORTH INDIAN CURRIES

Pat Chapman Founded the Curry Club in 1982. A regular broadcaster on television and radio, he is the author of 20 books, which have sold more than 1 million copies.

GRILLS AND BARBECUES

Brian Turner Chef/patron of Turner's in Knightsbridge and one of Britain's most popular food broadcasters; he appears frequently on *Ready Steady Cook, Food and Drink* and many other television programmes.

SUMMER AND WINTER CASSEROLES

Anton Edelmann Maître Chef des Cuisines at the Savoy Hotel, London. Author of six cookery books, he has also appeared on television.

TRADITIONAL PUDDINGS

Tessa Bramley Chef/patron of the acclaimed Old Vicarage restaurant in Ridgeway, Derbyshire and author of *The Instinctive Cook*.

DECORATED CAKES

Jane Asher Author of several cookery books and a novel. She has also appeared in her own television series, *Jane Asher's Christmas* (1995).

FAVOURITE CAKES

Mary Berry One of Britain's leading cookery writers, her numerous books include *Mary Berry's Ultimate Cake Book*. She has made many television and radio appearances.

ICE CREAMS AND SEMI FREDDI

Ann and Franco Taruschio Owners of the renowned Walnut Tree Inn near Abergavenny in Wales, soon to appear in a television series, *Franco and Friends: Food from the Walnut Tree*. They have written three books together.

Photographs © Philip Wilkins 1997

First published in 1997 by
George Weidenfeld & Nicolson
The Orion Publishing Group
Orion House
5 Upper St Martin's Lane
London WC2H 9EA

British Library Cataloguing-in-Publication data
A catalogue record for this book is available from
the British Library

ISBN 0 297 82336 1

Designed by Lucy Holmes
Edited by Maggie Ramsay
Food styling by Louise Pickford
Typesetting by Tiger Typeset